How to Make Money Online using AI

Everything you Need to Know About Artificial Intelligence to Make You Rich

MATTHEW RYMER HARRISON

D1707576

Disclaimer:

This book is an informational resource only and should not be considered investment advice or a recommendation to invest in artificial intelligence. The author and publisher make no warranty of any kind with respect to the accuracy or completeness of the information presented in this book.

Furthermore, the author and publisher shall not be liable for any loss or damage caused by reliance on the information contained in this book. It is important that readers do their own research and make their own decisions regarding their investments in artificial intelligence.

It is important to note that past performance is not indicative of future results and that performance in the field of artificial intelligence can be highly volatile. Therefore, readers are advised to consult a financial advisor before making any investment decisions in artificial intelligence.

Please note that this book may include affiliate links. This means that the author may receive a commission for purchases made through such links. This will not affect the price paid by the reader, but helps support the creation of future informational resources.

By reading this book, readers accept this disclaimer and assume full responsibility for their own investment decisions.

Acknowledgments

I want to begin by thanking all the pioneers in the field of artificial intelligence who have opened new frontiers in technology and demonstrated the potential of AI to transform society. Without their vision and dedication, this book would not exist.

I also want to thank my team, who have worked tirelessly to help me achieve my goals in the AI field. Together, we have proven that it is possible to make money with AI, and I hope to inspire more people to join us in this exciting adventure.

Last but not least, I want to thank all the readers of this book, especially those new to the field of AI. It is my hope that my story and strategies will give you the motivation and tools you need to take advantage of this unique opportunity for financial freedom. Together, we can help more people achieve independence and build a better future for everyone.

Dedication

I dedicate this book to all people who struggle to achieve their freedom and seek a more fulfilling life. This book is for those who are willing to learn and take action to achieve their dreams, and for those who believe in the power of artificial intelligence to transform their lives.

The truth

"The truth is that the countries with the highest robot density - South Korea, Germany, Japan - have the lowest unemployment rates". Ulrich Spiesshofer.

Own translation: the truth is that the most robot-dense countries - South Korea, Germany, Japan - have the lowest unemployment rates.

I will never forget my impression when I discovered that Artificial Intelligence (AI) was already doing jobs better than people. One of my passions is writing and to expand my books to other markets. At a certain point I decided to translate some of them. I started with English and hired a professional translator.

I paid him, sent him the texts and, after several weeks (sometimes even months) I had them back in Shakespeare's language. Although I am not 100% fluent in the language, I have a sufficient level to hold conversations, read books, watch movies... and proofread translations.

The truth is that my "dear" translator made quite a few mistakes. Some of them were typos, lifelong typos. We are human, we make mistakes. Others were more serious. Despite having their titles and so on.

The translation task is really complex since two languages are not the same. One word is not entirely equivalent to another. More than translators, sometimes what they are is adapters, it is an art that requires a great deal of knowledge.

That was my experience with translations: expensive, slow, and not very good.

Until one day I met DeepL, an AI that translates texts (even entire files) in a matter of seconds and with impressive quality.

The paid version even allows you to choose whether you want formal or informal language.

It is not perfect. For example, it happens that in Spanish it is not necessary for the subject to be explicit. I can write: vive en Madrid. Without saying whether the subject is he or she. The problem when translating a sentence like "vive en Madrid" is that in English you need a subject (he or she) and since you don't have it, you must use the context to know the gender (masculine or feminine), this information is not always there.

Therefore, even AI makes mistakes.

But, in my experience, it beats the average translator hands down. It totally revolutionizes the industry. And the same goes for other professions. This is changing the world and this book is made for you not to be left behind.

Let me give you a little more detail on this case so that you are aware of the magnitude of the change. A more or less long book can cost you thousands of euros to translate and you will have to wait for months.

With DeepL (perhaps with other AI-based translation software as well) you can get the same job done in a matter of seconds and at ridiculously low costs. It costs you virtually nothing to do an AI translation.

If you use the aforementioned translator you can enjoy a free trial in which it allows you to change languages up to twenty files in a month. That is: you enter a text file and it returns it to you in the language you select.

In addition, you could also translate texts by copying and pasting them into the web, infinitely.

When the free trial runs out, if you want to continue translating without paying a cent, just change your data: another name, another email and another card. You will be able to create new accounts and continue using the free trial until you get bored (or you are so grateful that you decide to use the paid version, perhaps with the benefits it has generated without paying).

AI is a controversial topic. There are those who complain about it. As already happened during the industrial era with Luddism, a workers' movement against machines, changes generate resistance.

But progress is unstoppable. We know this process as creative destruction, as Joseph Schumpeter, Austrian economist, explained it.

AI is killing many jobs, in addition to traditional translators, it also threatens graphic designers and writers, among others.

The world is changing.

And, as C. Darwin said, it is not the strongest that survives: it is the one that best adapts to the environment.

I congratulate you for reading this book, you are an enterprising person with a great future ahead of you.

Here you have the instruction manual, the map. But nothing will change in your reality if you don't act. Implement what you will learn in these pages and your life will never be the same.

Translators, designers and writers are not going to disappear, they just have new tools.

Don't fight against progress, use it to your advantage.

Today these professionals must supervise AI, that's their job. At least of those who have been able to adapt.

Ever since I became aware of the potential of this technology, I have been obsessed with getting the most out of it.

That is why I have spent the last few years researching and experimenting. This book is the result of many trials and errors. It is the manual that I would have liked to find when I started.

Enjoy it and, above all, use it to bring value to the world and make money from it.

Community and welcome gift

If you want to be part of this libertarian project and get the next free *ebooks* as soon as we publish them, join the channel on Telegram:

"The future will belong to artificial intelligence and the first country to master it will be the ruler of the world." Vladimir Putin.

What AI really is and how you can make money with it

There is a lot of confusion about what AI is and how it works. What differentiates this technology is its ability to learn automatically (known as *machine learning*).

Let me give you an example. A phone or a computer, which offers you limited options, and does not take into account what happens to change, has no AI.

In contrast, a multitude of platforms that you have been using for a long time have AI. Netflix, YouTube and Jeff Bezos' company are able to show you content based on your experience, based on what you have watched and what you have rejected. They learn from you and your behavior to improve their selection. That's AI.

They used to say that the value of going to a traditional bookstore or video store (as opposed to the world's largest market place and Netflix or similar platforms) is that they knew you and could make personalized recommendations.

Today it seems that AI knows you better than anyone else.

And how to make money with AI? There are many ways. Some more indirect, like using those marketplaces that already have the technology built in, posting content on Jeff Bezos' company or YouTube.

And other more direct ones, such as being an AI programmer, investing in shares of companies in the sector, offering related services or products.

Let's start with the tool that has become most famous... Open IA's GPT Chat.

ChatGPT

As the name itself says, chat means conversation, it is a program capable of writing as if it were a person. One with access to a lot of information and with that key ingredient that distinguishes AI: the ability to learn.

What do the now famous acronyms stand for? Generative Pre-trained Transformer.

Technically, it is a natural language processing (NLP) model based on the learning technique that gives its name to its last letter: Transformer.

It has been trained with millions of parameters and texts to make it capable of giving "intelligent" answers.

Its source code is available on GitHUB (do not modify or distribute).

Behind it is Open AI, a company dedicated to AI research and development founded in 2015 by, among others, Elon Musk, the famous owner and developer of, among other projects, Tesla, Twitter, Neuralink and Space X.

In theory Open IA is non-profit and open to integration with applications, what we know as API: application programming interface.

That is: they make it easier for them to use ChatGPT technology. Although this comes at a cost.

Currently you can use this tool for free from https://openai.com/blog/chatgpt/, you only need to register with an email and a password (they are not verifying accounts by phone or with official identification). They offer a free version, although sometimes it is not available, supposedly because the number of users exceeds them.

In fact, the numbers said they were losing money in huge amounts. Since very recently they also offer a paid version with a monthly subscription for about twenty dollars that allows you to avoid being left without use in times of system congestion, shorter response times and priority access to new features and improvements.

Subscribers will receive:

* General access to ChatGPT, even during peak times

* Faster response times

* Priority access to new features and improvements

Step 1: Go to this address: https://openai.com/blog/chatgpt/, you can Google gpt chat to go, note that the domain is openai.com.

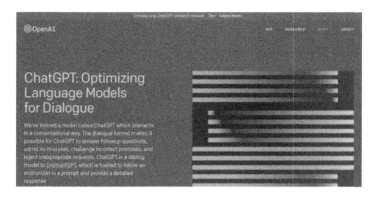

Step 2: At the bottom left you will find TRY GPT. Click or tap there.

Step 3. If you don't have an account yet, it's time to create one, choose Sign up. If you already have one, or when you do: Log in.

Welcome to ChatGPT

Log in with your OpenAI account to continue

Log in   Sign up

Step 4. In the bottom right bar you can ask ChatGPT whatever you want. Note that you should review the results and edit them if necessary. You can always ask it to rewrite, to rewrite in another language or to make any variations you want. Next, we will see in more detail how to make money with ChatGPT. **The key is the information you give it.** At the moment you are not connected to the Internet and you "only" have the data provided to you in 2021 (you have nothing later), that's a big limit to your knowledge.

What is ChatGPT for? It makes summaries, lists, answers all kinds of questions, creates texts according to your indications, asks you questions if you ask it...

What are its advantages and strengths?

If you learn to write what we know as *prompts*, that text from which it responds, its potential can be impressive.

Link it to your learning. It takes context into account, so the more information you give it the more accurate it becomes.

It is capable of solving tests that would qualify it to be a doctor, seems resourceful and, while not perfect, has so far proven to be the first massively AI chat in history.

In the first five days it already had one million users, the same number that Facebook and Instagram took years to reach. Today, although not much time has passed yet, it already has many, many millions of users worldwide. This is one of the main advantages as it can help its development. They are collecting all the information they receive, so never reveal anything confidential.

Having such a large number of customers (today it is already generating money with the subscription), together with a very powerful human team behind it, are a certain guarantee that in the future it will continue to improve and become more and more powerful.

It offers many options: automatic customer service chat, review of scientific articles, creation of programming code, data analysis, plan generation...

What are the disadvantages and risks?

It does not yet offer texts of the highest quality. At least in most cases or part of the text. In my experience they can serve as a basis, but you should review and modify them because they make common mistakes such as redundancies, repeating structures and words excessively.

We do not yet know how the regulation will be in this regard and whether it can be detected. For example, there is a lot of talk about creating content for web pages with ChatGPT, will Google penalize it?

According to official sources, the important thing is that the content responds to search intentions.

If you run a ChatGPT text through a plagiarism detector (I have), it will tell you that it is original content.

However, what would happen if someone did the same *prompt*?

Let's take an example, you want an article about chatGPT and you write to it:

Give me an article about chatGPT.

If someone else writes (wrote or will write) the same thing, you may get a similar text.

Google does penalize publishing content that is already available on another website. It is considered that you are not respecting intellectual property rights, copyright. If Google finds that the content of your website is elsewhere, you will not rank on their first page.

You will be less visible than cryptocurrencies.

Another risk is that the system will collapse, be banned or fail.

It is worth mentioning that there are other more interesting text creation AIs that we will see in this book.

Another risk worth mentioning is if you use ChatGPT to create books that you will publish in the world's largest marketplace. There have already been account closures (with all that entails, such as not getting paid outstanding royalties) for creating AI texts.

The question is whether they can detect it. In my opinion, the best thing to do is to use other *software*: Write it. And always provide your own content. Your story, your experience, the AI doesn't have that.

Better opportunities to earn money:

The first thing: whatever the use, you must understand how to write it to get the best results.

The first rule: the more precision, the better.

Let's say you want a text for your social network. Include information about the target audience, everything you want to appear, how you want the text to be structured (*bullets points*)...

Also, if it is something complex, you can do it in several *prompts*.

I'm going to show you, let's say I'm working on *marketing* for a hair salon.

I am writing to you:

What are the desires and pain points of potential hairdressing salon customers in Spain?

And he answers me:

Some of the desires and pain points that potential clients of a hairdressing salon in Spain may have include:

Wishes:

Look for a current haircut according to your personal taste and style.
Find a hairdresser that offers a professional and quality service.
Have a pleasant and relaxing experience at the salon.
Personalized advice on hair care and maintenance.

Pain points:

Problems with previous hairdressers who have not met your expectations.

Not finding a suitable schedule for your availability.
Concern for service cost and quality.
Fear of leaving unsatisfied with the result of the haircut.

It is important to take these customer desires and pain points into account in order to provide a service that meets their expectations and provides them with a positive experience. Some aspects that may be valued include flexible hours, reasonable prices, a professional and trained staff, and a welcoming and relaxing environment.

My next *prompt* is:

With those desires and pain points in mind, I want a text to post on the business's instagram, I would like it to be persuasive, follow the AIDA formula, have bullet points and end with a call to action

And what it has given me is:

Here is a text that follows the AIDA formula and meets the requirements you have indicated:

Are you looking for a salon where you can find the perfect haircut for you? At [salon name], we offer you the beauty experience you need!

Attention:

We strive to provide you with a professional and quality service.
We offer flexible schedules to fit your schedule.
We have a highly trained and friendly team.

Interest:

You'll want to experience the difference in our relaxing and welcoming environment.
Take advantage of our personalized advice for the care and maintenance of your hair.
Forget your worries about cost and quality, we offer fair prices and impressive results.

Desire:

Want to look and feel beautiful with the haircut of your dreams?
Do you want a pleasant and carefree salon experience?

Action:

Schedule your appointment with us today! At [name of salon] we are here to make your beauty wishes come true, we are waiting for you!

This text combines the desires and pain points I mentioned previously with the AIDA formula to create an engaging and persuasive message for your Instagram followers. Plus, at the end it includes a clear and direct call to action to invite your followers to take action and schedule an appointment with you.

As you can see, it is not a text that would be convenient to just copy and paste. To optimize the use of ChatGPT and make money, edit it. In this case you should delete the introduction and the conclusions, as well as when it says Attention, Interest, Development and Action (these words are the AIDA formula but they do not need to appear explicitly, it is a guide to structure the text).

I would also delete some of the *bullet points* (the dots that appear before the text), add bold, icons and *hashtags*.

This way in a few minutes you can have a high quality text for a social network.

Having explained the process in one of the simplest cases, let's see how you can earn money with ChatGPT.

Completing the example: one option is to use it to create content, either for your own business or for others.

In order not to get lost among infinite possibilities, you can look at it in the following way: products or services.

Although it is a false dilemma, you can create products and services, you should be clear about the difference so that you can design a strategy according to your objectives.

The advantage of selling products over the Internet is that the scalability is brutal and, once the product is created and put on sale, it can be very passive.

The advantage of selling services is that you can provide more value and therefore charge more.

An example of selling products is to make a blog (with articles created with AI) in which you deal with a niche market with affiliation to the largest marketplace in the world. It could be books, furniture, jewelry, cell phones... The number of items sold by the giant with the smile and fast home delivery is the limit.

If instead you want to sell services, you could also make a blog, but where you have organic advertising of your own services. Organic advertising means that you sell without being noticed. Are you a personal trainer, trainer, therapist...? You create content for your audience and end with a call to action for them to leave you their contact details (it can be in exchange for a free gift, such as an ebook or a free call).

We can summarize the possibilities in four main groups:

- Content creation: academic papers, articles, books, social media posts, video scripts...

- Translations.

- Persuasive writing (*copywriting*): sales pages, product descriptions in Jeff Bezos' company, *landing pages*, *email marketing...*

- Programming. You can review, create or review code.

It is also possible to use its technology as a chatbot to automatically respond to customers, but this use does not seem so revolutionary to me because there were and are already effective AI alternatives. It is a relatively simple task to respond according to certain parameters and leave a way to communicate with a human in case the bot cannot solve.

Let's elaborate a little more on each of the four options before moving on to the next tool.

We start from the first dilemma: selling products or services?

If you want to sell products you will have to publish your writings, you can do it on your website or through books on platforms such as KDP, D2D, Lulu or Etsy.
Warning: although as far as I know it is not forbidden to do it with artificial intelligence, there seem to be cases of KDP accounts closed for using AI, so be careful. Make it very difficult to perceive that it has been (partly) created automatically.
With precise *prompts* and by editing the results, plus adding some personal parts.
There are already programs to detect AI, such as this one: https://www.zerogpt.com/.

If you are interested in this topic of self-publishing books, I recommend *Vive del cuento thanks to the ICME method*. You should focus on creating a differentiated brand and that you will reap the rewards in the long run, when you have built an audience thanks to a series of books.

Focus on making books of the highest quality possible.

My first recommendation is that, if you have not already done so, you should create an account in Draft2Digital to self-publish books for free. From my experience it is the best way to generate passive income with books and at the end of the book I will explain how you can do it step by step. Here you have the QR code:

The book self-publishing business has in Jeff Bezos' company its Achilles heel, most of the books are sold in its store almost all self-publishers only publish in it.

KDP is the name of the self-publishing platform for books at Jeff Bezos' company.

The business of many self-publishers has disappeared from one day to the next because they violate some rule and their accounts are closed.

And, although not yet a standard, the use of AI could become prohibited.

How do you avoid the dreaded danger of the world's largest marketplace closing your account?

With D2D.

By publishing on D2D you will also be publishing on Jeff Bezos' company, but without the risk of the *ecommerce* giant closing your account. It is impossible because you do not have an account with them. The most they could do to you is to block a book in case they consider that it is violating any rule.

The other option, if you don't want to self-publish, is to sell that content. To do this you can make accounts on social networks, web and enter *freelance marketplaces* such as Fiverr, UpWork, Workana and Freelancer.

There are also sites for students who want someone to do their homework, especially in English, some of them are: UvoCorp, Ace-MyHomework and Academic.

If you want ChatGPT to create content in another language, it is not necessary that you also use it, it is enough that in the *promp* you include the indication that it does it in English. Putting "in English" at the end of the text is usually enough for it to be understood; you could also state at the beginning of the conversation: "I am going to write to you in Spanish, I want you to write to me in English, understand?

If you are going to do translations the other option is the platform already mentioned: DeepL. Is ChatGPT or DeepL better? This is a difficult question. In my experience both offer good results, but they are different. If you want to translate a text, DeepL is exactly that. ChatGPT allows you to communicate and ask for texts in other languages, even if you don't have them yet.

You can use ChatGPT for title, subtitle and description of the book. And DeepL for the translation of the full text file (something ChatGPT does not do).

How to make money with translations? As with the content creation seen in the previous point, you can choose whether to publish or sell it.

This option is the one in the example we made showing how it works. Remember to include information about the target audience for a more effective result. Copywriting, also known as *copywriting* or persuasive writing, is a highly valued skill in the market that is sometimes misunderstood. There are many trainings on the subject that pretend to teach you supposed secrets that are no longer so. Here I am going to summarize what I consider essential for you to know in order to be successful when using ChatGPT to create this type of texts:

Know well who you are addressing, what are the benefits they are looking for, what words and expressions do they use? What are their fears and pains? What are their desires? The text should feel like a friend talking to you to help you.

The description should be based on benefits. Give them a mental picture of the outcome you are selling, of what life will be like with the product or service you are talking about.

Tell them a story they empathize with. We learn and remember stories because they move us. That's the key, show your vulnerability, that you are someone human, like the one who reads you, that's how you will connect and leave a mark (remember that the word mark means that: what remains when you leave). Use the "save the cat" technique: start with a scene in which you show your selfless generosity in a difficult moment.

If you are interested in this marketing topic I recommend *THE HONOR METHOD: THE DEFINITIVE GUIDE TO ACHIEVE FINANCIAL FREEDOM WITH DIGITAL MARKETING AND ONLINE BUSINESS*. Writing all kinds of texts is a very powerful skill that AI has just democratized. But don't forget that no one can guarantee you the results, to undertake is to take responsibility. My recommendation is that you edit your texts, adding personal touches. That editing is where you will make the difference with those who do not make an effort and end up being marginalized from the market for providing little (or no) value.

Before I finish talking about Chat GPT I want to show you his answer when I asked him to help me with the creation of this book, here is his explanation:

There are many ways artificial intelligence can be used to make money. Here are some of the most common ways:

Data analytics: Artificial intelligence can help analyze large amounts of data to identify patterns and trends, which can be valuable to businesses and organizations.

Task automation: Artificial intelligence can be used to automate repetitive and tedious tasks, saving time and money.

Product development: Artificial intelligence can be used to develop innovative products, such as virtual assistants, recommender systems and smart toys.

Cloud services: Companies can offer AI-based services through the cloud, allowing customers to access the technology without having to invest in expensive hardware and software.

Ads and marketing: Artificial intelligence can help companies personalize their marketing messages and ads for each customer, increasing effectiveness and ROI.

These are just a few examples of how artificial intelligence can be used to make money. However, it is important to keep in mind that, as with any technology, there are also challenges and ethical concerns to consider.

To further refine the answer I asked for webs (still aware that it is limited to 2021):

There are many websites that focus on using artificial intelligence to make money online, but here are some of the most important ones:

Kaggle: Kaggle is a community of data scientists and artificial intelligence developers who compete in challenges and contests to solve practical, real-world problems.

H2O.ai: H2O.ai provides machine learning and data analytics solutions in the cloud for businesses and organizations.

OpenAI: OpenAI is an artificial intelligence research organization that seeks to build technologies that advance humanity.

NVIDIA NGC: NVIDIA NGC is a cloud platform for artificial intelligence that provides access to pre-trained models, tools and deep learning technologies.

Coursera: Coursera is an online education platform that offers courses in artificial intelligence and machine learning, as well as online certificates and degree programs.

These are just a few examples of websites that focus on the use of artificial intelligence to make money online.

However, it is important to keep in mind that there is no "magic formula" for making money with artificial intelligence, and that it requires a combination of technical knowledge, business skills and a clear and strategic vision.

Keep in mind when using ChatGTP that the key is to train him with relevant information. You don't have to limit yourself to giving him the data you think are the most important, you can ask him to ask you questions in order to give you more relevant answers.

ChatGTP can even serve as a trainer, *coach*, motivator, therapist, psychologist...

AI changes life especially when we connect it with virtual reality. virtual reality? I'm referring to what recently became fashionable to call metaverse, since Facebook that became Meta maybe, although it's already passed into oblivion, who knows when you read this.

Everything is evolving so fast that this book will soon be a historical chronicle of the beginning of the massive use of AI.

Remember that ChatGPT is made to integrate with applications. This is what we know as API and what other AIs also offer.

Escribelo.ia

To continue with the topic of text creation with AI I am going to tell you about escribelo.ia, a little known Spanish alternative. Still.

This AI does not have a free version but the cheapest one is only 19 € per month for a maximum of 20 thousand words. If you choose the annual option it would be 15 € per month. In addition you get 10 thousand more if you sign up from my affiliate link:

And you can get more with bonuses offered to you once you're in.

Let's see if you are interested...

Escribelo is focused on SEO Copywriting. But the "Article Generator" is not your only option. Its interface is very user-friendly and with different options depending on what text you want it to generate.

As if you were on a freelancers page looking for someone to solve an assignment, with the difference that you have it in seconds.

I'm going to show you a little bit. This is the image that you will find at the entrance, the *home in* the Anglo-Saxon jargon.

If you click on the pricing section you have options up to 149 euros per month for 300,000 words and custom options (for companies).

Once you have an account you will be able to choose from numerous features in addition to creating articles, such as summaries, article ideas, listings, meta titles and meta descriptions for SEO...

It has integrations (API) with Chrome, WordPress, Notion... and are open to user requests.

I'm going to show you his answer to one of the research questions in this book:

What are the main Artificial Intelligence software to make money with and how do they work?

The use of Artificial Intelligence (AI) can be seen in various fields, such as the implementation of automated process robotics (APR), the open source machine learning platform H2O and Natural Language Processing (NLP), which allows machines to understand human language. RPA is a method of automating administrative tasks that can help companies save time and free up resources for other tasks. H2O is a machine learning tool that helps companies identify and anticipate the behavior of their users. Finally, NLP allows users to interact with a simulated 3D environment. These AI tools can help companies improve their efficiency and increase their profits.

AI is also often used in everyday life, such as the Siri voice assistant in iOS. This technology is used for activities such as content marketing, content generation, email marketing, social media marketing and lead generation, among others. These AI softwares allow companies to have a variety of tools to improve their productivity, and thus, reap greater rewards.

Introduction to Artificial Intelligence

Advanced programming, such as Artificial Intelligence (AI), allows users to interact with a simulated environment in a full 360-degree environment. This technology is used in a variety of fields, from marketing to content creation and data analysis to online advertising. Here are some of the top AI software solutions available to businesses to help them generate revenue.

Robotic Process Automation (RPA) decreases the time and effort required for administrative tasks. H2O is an open source platform for machine learning. Finally, natural language processing allows machines to understand human language. These three AI applications are beneficial for monetization in areas such as automation, marketing, advertising and data analytics.

Common Business Uses of Artificial Intelligence

Robotic Process Automation (RPA): Robotic Process Automation (RPA) is an administrative process automation tool that allows companies to manage and execute processes more easily and efficiently. This technology optimizes business processes, reducing waiting times and improving productivity. It is one of the most common applications of Artificial Intelligence in the business world.

H2O: H2O is an open source machine learning platform that enables companies to build, train and test predictive models. This platform provides various machine learning algorithms, such as deep neural networks, decision trees and logistic regression. These models can be used to optimize decision making, forecast sales and improve process efficiency.

Natural Language Processing: Natural Language Processing allows machines to understand human language. This technology is used to perform customer sentiment analysis, classify content, understand document content and other uses. This tool is useful for improving user experience and brand interaction.

Types of Artificial Intelligence

Technological advances have enabled companies to reap huge benefits. This is due to a range of AI software that provides solutions and tools to improve productivity and competitiveness. Robotic Process Automation (RPA) enables automation of administrative processes, while H2O is an open source platform for implementing machine learning algorithms. Natural Language Processing (NLP) enables machines to understand human language.

AI software can be used to generate revenue, such as in content marketing, online advertising, lead generation, chatbot creation, email marketing and social media optimization. These AI programs help reduce costs, increase efficiency and boost sales. On the other hand, the use of these tools requires a high level of expertise and a considerable initial investment, so a qualified professional is recommended.

Artificial Intelligence in Everyday Life

Artificial Intelligence (AI) is a form of computer programming that allows users to interact with a 360-degree simulated environment. This technology has been widely deployed in everyday life to help professionals make money efficiently. Leading software solutions that use AI to generate profits include Robotic Process

Automation (RPA), H2O and Natural Language Processing (NLP).

In addition to these software solutions, AI has also been widely employed in everyday life to help users perform common tasks. A great example of this is Siri, Apple's voice assistant. AI is a powerful tool that helps businesses run more efficiently and save money.

AI software solutions can be used effectively to generate benefits, provided that the fundamentals of the technology are understood and the right equipment is available for implementation. This technology is an excellent way to track business processes and save resources.

In conclusion, Artificial Intelligence is a valuable asset for those looking to make money intelligently and efficiently. With the right knowledge and configuration, AI solutions can help companies increase profits and reduce costs.

Benefits of Artificial Intelligence in Businesses

Technology has been playing an increasingly important role in the business world, and Artificial Intelligence (AI) is no exception. With the help of AI, organizations can save time and resources while improving efficiency. Robotic Process Automation (RPA), H2O and Natural Language Processing (NLP) are some of the main AI tools that can help generate revenue.

RPA enables companies to automate mundane tasks such as data collection, document management and billing.

H2O is an open source platform for machine learning that allows users to create, deploy and refine learning models. Finally, NLP enables machines to understand human language for tasks such as speech recognition. All of these AI technologies offer businesses the ability to increase efficiency and create new opportunities to generate revenue.

Conclusion

The use of advanced technology is essential for companies to remain competitive and generate more wealth. Artificial Intelligence is a powerful tool that can be employed to automate tedious tasks and optimize profits. RPA, H2O and natural language processing are three of the main AI approaches that can be used to facilitate workflows and create content more efficiently. AI can be used for a variety of tasks, such as email campaigns, content writing and marketing efforts. By leveraging AI, companies can stay ahead of the competition and achieve success. As technology continues to evolve, the importance of AI in generating revenue is only increasing.

What do you think? You can compare it with the ChatGPT text. The difference is that here we have an AI connected to the Internet and therefore up to date, plus the input of information, the *prompt*, here is limited.

Escríbelo has been trained by Spanish copywriters and is especially effective for the Hispanic market.

What it asks you for is the title of the article, the keywords, if you want it to be medium (500-1000) or long (1000 -2500 words), this is what they recommend for very competitive niches) and if you want it to be formal or informal (by default it is informal).

Let's see more.

I'm going to ask you for a new article, about themselves. The one I showed you was long. Now I am going to ask you for a short one. The keywords I use are: seo, make money online, artificial intelligence, ia, business, entrepreneurship. This is the result:

How to make money with Escribelo.ai? The Best Step-by-Step Guide, Strengths or Advantages and Weaknesses or Risks

The term **Escribelo.ai** can be associated with the task of writing a perfect textual content in Spanish language using artificial intelligence. To do so, it is necessary to develop a learning process using a combination of natural language programming and machine learning strategies. This process usually consists of three basic steps: the first, which consists of outlining the objective of the text, the second, which adds the personal touch, and finally, the generation of the unique content. Although this technology has become very popular, especially in business and advertising, people are still wondering if there is a reliable way to make money with it.

According to a survey conducted, it has been found that

due to **artificial intelligence (AI)**, many online companies now have the ability to offer unique solutions for businesses and entrepreneurs. So, the question is, can we make money with Escribelo.ai? The answer is yes, and in this article we will explain why and the best steps to make money with this technology.

What is Escribelo.ai?

Escribelo.ai is an advanced content writing application based on artificial intelligence and natural language programming. It is designed with the purpose of simplifying and automating the task of writing any type of textual content, such as articles, blog posts, promotions, advertisements or marketing materials. This application is easy to use and includes a wide range of features and tools.

How can we earn money with Escribelo.ai?

The first step to making money with this technology is to map out a goal for the textual content and then determine a target audience. This is essential to ensure that the content is valuable and engaging. Once the target is identified, you can start making money with Escribelo.ai. Here are some of the ways to use this technology and make a profit:

Freelance writing:

Freelancers are using Escribelo.ai to improve the writing process and provide companies and organizations with high quality texts. This is a great opportunity to monetize your content and gain more visibility.

Internet marketing:

Internet marketers are using this technology to create amazing content that is SEO-friendly, engaging and well-structured.

Translation Services:

This technology has proven to be an excellent tool for translations of any type of language. It is useful for translating documents, articles and promotions in different languages.

Create eBooks and White Papers:

eBooks and white papers are excellent tools for making money and Escribelo.ai can help you create content for them quickly and easily.

Advantages and Disadvantages of Escribelo.ai

Like any technology, Escribelo.ai has both advantages and disadvantages. Here we will mention some of the main ones:

Advantages:

Friendly, simple and intuitive interface.

Automation of the writing process.

Possibility of creating UIs (user interface).

Wide range of functionalities.

Write content in different languages.

Disadvantages:

It is still in the early stages of development, so there are a limited number of options.

The content created is not 100% unique and has not been reviewed.

Content is not always tailored to the target audience.

Conclusion

Making money with Escribelo.ai is a great opportunity for entrepreneurs looking for a way to monetize their content. This technology can be used in different ways, such as freelancing, Internet marketing, translation or creation of eBooks and whitepapers. The advantages of using this technology include a user-friendly interface, automation of the writing process, a wide range of features and writing in different languages. However, there are certain disadvantages such as lack of features and lack of uniqueness in the content generated. All in all, Escríbelo.ai can be of great help to anyone who wants to earn money quickly and efficiently.

Interesting?

I would add among the advantages of Escribelo.ia its support, from the web with a click, and its Telegram group.

It also offers image creation, up to 50 images per month for those who have the minimum payment plan. Here I share with you one that I generated with the title of this book:

The issue is what business you want to use AI for. Escribelo.ia is perfect if you want to create blog articles, and it can also be very useful for YouTube video scripts, product descriptions in Jeff Bezos' company or other ecommerce.

As always, you can decide whether you are going to sell your services or you are going to sell products. In either case, the time and/or money you save with this AI makes it worth it.

Nowadays the difference with ChatGPT is very big. With Open IA's child, it is rare that you could publish a paragraph without editing it, but with Escribelo.ia the text is much more successful.

If you compare the price with what it would cost you to hire the service or dedicate the time to it, for me there is no doubt.

The best opportunity to make money with Escribelo.ia is to blog and/or sell writing services.

The second could be to use it to write non-fiction books.

Before continuing with the analysis of other AIs, I would like to point out that the one we have just seen is the only Spanish one.

I leave you the QR code in case you are interested in taking advantage of the opportunity, remember that you have a five-day guarantee (if you are not convinced you can ask for a refund) and that if you do it from my link you will have 10 thousand extra words in addition to those that go with your plan:

Jasper AI

How does it work? This is another persuasive *copywriter*, his website is https://www.jasper.ai/. This is also known as Jarvis. Here is his *home page*:

You must open an account to get started, you can do it with your Google user in one click. It is a content creator with many functions as well, from writing the bio for your social network to emails, ads and -how not- articles for your blog.

Here the minimum price is higher than in Escríbelo: 59 dollars per month for about 50 thousand words (with Escríbelo it is 20 thousand words for 19 euros).

It is worth mentioning that the more words you buy, the cheaper they get (the price increase is not proportional). The next package from Escríbelo after the most basic one has just 50,000 words (the same as the cheapest one from Jasper) but the price is 39 € (much less than the 59 € the American asks for).

I have asked ChatGPT about how to make money with Jasper IA. To refine the answer I have incorporated a little more information for him so he can put himself in the shoes of the writer of this book. This is what we "talked" about:

I want you to write as if you were a well-known disseminator of knowledge about entrepreneurship and finance, motivational and didactic, is that okay?

Of course! I would love to help you understand the concepts of entrepreneurship and finance in a clear and motivating way.

Let's start with entrepreneurship. Being an entrepreneur means taking risks and having the vision and passion to create something new and unique. It is important to have a clear idea of what you want to achieve and how you plan to get there. It is also crucial to have an entrepreneurial mindset, that is, to be willing to continuously learn and improve, to be perseverant, and to be willing to make tough decisions when necessary.

Now let's talk about finance. Finances are a critical part of business success. It is important to have tight control of income and expenses, as well as to plan and monitor your budget effectively. In addition, it is important to have a solid understanding of how the financial markets work and how to invest wisely.

In summary, both entrepreneurship and finance require dedication, hard work and a positive mindset. But if you are willing to invest the necessary time and energy, you can achieve great things and reach your financial and business goals. Never lose motivation and keep going!

I want you to explain step by step how I can use Jasper AI to make money online. What are the advantages of this AI compared to ChatGPT, You.com and Escribelo.ia, what are its strengths, weaknesses and risks?

Sure, let's talk about how to use Jasper AI to make money online. Jasper AI is an artificial intelligence platform that allows users to create custom chatbots to interact with their customers or clients. Here are the basic steps to use Jasper AI to make money online:

Identify an online business opportunity that you can address through the use of a chatbot.

Create a Jasper IA account and learn how to use their platform to create and customize your chatbots.

Design and develop your chatbot, making sure it has the right features and functionality to address your business opportunity.

Implement your chatbot on your website or online platform and start promoting it and attracting users.

Monitor and analyze data from your chatbots to ensure they are performing effectively and generating revenue.

As for the advantages of Jasper IA compared to other artificial intelligence services such as ChatGPT, You.com and Escribelo.ia, one of the main advantages is its ease of use and intuitive interface, which means that even if you don't have a great deal of experience in technology, you can still create and use chatbots effectively. In addition, Jasper AI offers a wide range of features and functionalities, which means that you can customize your chatbots to suit your specific needs.

As for Jasper IA's strengths, its ease of use and wide range of features and functionalities are definitely two of its most outstanding strengths. It is also known for its reliability and its ability to integrate with other platforms and online services.

In terms of weaknesses, one of the biggest weaknesses of Jasper AI is that, like any other artificial intelligence service, it can be vulnerable to bugs or technical glitches. In addition, as an online platform, Jasper AI can also be vulnerable to online security risks, such as cyber attacks and data privacy.

In summary, Jasper AI is an effective and easy-to-use artificial intelligence platform that can help you generate online revenue by creating and using personal chatbots.

So chatbot, according to ChatGPT, is the way to make money with Jasper... Very interesting, is it true? Let's see what Write It thinks about the same. Incidentally I have also done a Google search to compare the result with what appears on the first web pages. I copy and paste as is (the title was given by me):

How to make money with Jasper IA? Step by step. Opportunities, challenges, weaknesses, risks and strengths.

In an increasingly digital world, Jasper IA is one of the latest and most useful technology tools for users who want to make money. It offers its users excellent ways to generate income consistently and securely. If you want to learn more about Jaspers AI staking technology, how to profit from its actions, opportunities, challenges, strengths and weaknesses, then read on!

What is Jasper AI?

Jasper AI is an artificial intelligence (AI) system developed to help users generate income safely and consistently through staking technology. This staking technology uses deep learning algorithms, based on Big Data, to make automatic recommendations for capital management. This opens up a variety of opportunities for users to generate income through coin or token staking.

How to make money using Jasper AI?

There are many ways users can make money using Jasper AI. Here are some of the main ways users can make money with the system:

Affiliate Marketing

Affiliate marketing is one of the easiest and most lucrative ways to make money online with Jasper AI. This is accomplished by following and recommending a variety of products to your followers to earn commissions if someone buys it.

Work from home

Currently, there are a variety of opportunities to work from home with Jasper AI, such as remote consulting, creating your own online store, trading, selling photos, freelance writing, home delivery, creating products and establishments named after successful series, among others.

Drug delivery market

The medication delivery market is an area that is usually tapped to make money, especially due to a large number of people with mobility issues or lack of time. Many people hire a delivery person to deliver medications to their home, which becomes a good opportunity to make money with Jasper AI.

Create a Youtube Channel

One of the best modern media is Youtube. If you can create quality content, it will attract views and these views will outperform conversion into advertising revenue. This means that it is a good opportunity to earn money with Jaspers AI staking technology.

Create your own professional blog

If you have the knowledge and skill to create a professional blog, then it is one of the best ways to make money with Jaspers AI. You can monetize your blog through different channels, such as ads, sponsored posts, affiliation, etc.

Advantages and disadvantages of using Jasper AI to make money

Before using any technology, it's important to consider the advantages and disadvantages of doing so. Here are some of the main advantages and disadvantages of using Jasper AI to make money:

Advantages

Steady income: Jaspers AI's staking technology allows for steady and stable revenue generation.

Safe: The algorithms used by Jaspers AI to predict the outcome of financial markets are incredibly safe and accurate.

Flexibility: There are a variety of ways and options to earn money with Jasper AI.

Disadvantages

Learning curve: As with any other software or tool, the learning curve for using the Jasper AI system may not be easy. It requires time and dedication.

Advanced technology: due to its advanced nature, technology needs a deep understanding in order to take advantage of it.

Conclusion

Jasper AI is a useful tool with which you can safely and stably earn money using staking technology. But, as with any digital tool, there are some inherent challenges in doing so. These include understanding the technology and deciding which is the best way to generate income. By considering these details, we are confident that Jasper AI will help you generate lucrative earnings.

This time it seems that Jasper has mixed AI with some cryptocurrency platform or similar. It is understandable that mistakes happen and what characterizes this technology is learning from them. As a user what you can do is contact support to report what happened. I was told that I had put a title that was too long.

Playground AI

is also a tool to be taken into account. It combines different functions in a different way to its competitors and with very competitive prices. It offers images as well as text. It uses Stable Diffusion technology and, in the paid version, also Dall-E.

Let's see what ChatGPT has to say:

in a didactic tone, tell me what a playground is, how it differs from chat gpt and how it can help a user to earn money (step by step).

Playground is an artificial intelligence platform that offers users the opportunity to experiment and play with different AI models to see how they can help them in their work or day-to-day lives.

Unlike ChatGPT, which is a particular language model, Playground allows you to test different AI models to find the one that best suits your needs. This means you can experiment with different AI solutions to see which one works best for you.

As for how it can help you make money, here are the basic steps for using Playground to increase your income:

Register with Playground and familiarize yourself with its platform and AI models.
Identify what problems or challenges in the business or financial world you are trying to address.
Use Playground's AI models to help you address these challenges and generate new business opportunities.
Monitor results and adjust your strategies accordingly to maximize your revenue.

In short, Playground is an artificial intelligence platform that offers users the opportunity to experiment and play with different AI models to find the one that best suits their needs. By following these basic steps, you can use

Playground to generate new business opportunities and increase your online revenue.

What are Playground's strengths, weaknesses and risks? What is the biggest opportunity it offers and how to take advantage of it? Tell me what the plan would be like for an entrepreneur who is just starting out and wants to make a lot of money with the internet using artificial intelligence.

Playground's strengths include the ability to experiment with different AI models and find the one that best suits your needs, as well as the ability to use artificial intelligence to address challenges and generate new business opportunities.

Some weaknesses of Playground include the need for prior technical knowledge to effectively use the platform and the possibility that results may not always be accurate or satisfactory.

In terms of risks, it is important to keep in mind that, as with any technology, there is some risk associated with the use of artificial intelligence. For example, there is the risk of information being leaked or misused, or the risk that the results will not be accurate or will not meet your expectations.

The biggest opportunity that Playground offers is the possibility of using artificial intelligence to address challenges and generate new business opportunities. To take advantage of this opportunity, it is important to research and experiment with different AI models and find the one that best suits your needs.

The plan for an entrepreneur who is just starting out and wants to make a lot of money with the internet using artificial intelligence could include the following steps:

Register with Playground and familiarize yourself with its platform and AI models.
Research and experiment with different AI models to find the one that best suits your needs.
Identifies challenges or opportunities in the business or financial world that can be addressed with the help of artificial intelligence.
Use Playground's AI models to address these challenges and generate new business opportunities.
Monitor your results and adjust your strategies accordingly to maximize your revenue.

In short, Playground is an artificial intelligence platform that offers entrepreneurs the opportunity to experiment and play with different AI models to find the one that best suits their needs. By following a strategic plan and monitoring your results, you can use artificial intelligence to address challenges and generate new business opportunities and eventually increase your online revenue.

It is quite an interesting text, but let's remember the limitation of ChatGPT: it is not connected to the Internet nor updated since 2021 (at least at the time of writing this book). Therefore, to complement the information, I use Write it. I put Playground, instead of Playground AI, and it made me an article about playgrounds. I added AI and shortened the subtitle to be more precise.Here is the result:

How to make money with Playground AI

One of the many advantages of Playground AI is its ability to help you make money. For those looking to supplement their income, or even make it a full-time career, Playground AI provides a vehicle to turn your ideas into a viable business. In this article, we'll discuss the various ways you can leverage Playground AI's tools and resources to generate a steady stream of additional income, as well as offer tips on how to maximize your profits and become a successful Playground AI entrepreneur.

Using Playground AI for affiliate marketing

Affiliate marketing is one of the most popular ways to make money with Playground AI and involves promoting products and services through various website links that, when clicked, earn you a commission. By leveraging Playground AI's powerful marketing platform, you can start promoting products and services related to your niche and quickly build a solid income stream. There are a few affiliate networks you can join for free, such as Jeff Bezos' company, Clickbank and Commission Junction.

Creative ways to monetize your content

In addition to affiliate marketing, you can also use Playground AI technology to create and monetize your own content. With AI-based content creation tools, you can create custom blogs, video channels and even podcasts to generate revenue. You can also use Playground AI's machine learning algorithms to create engaging social media campaigns and ads to further monetize your content. With Playground AI's AI-backed analytics, you can gain insights into your revenue potential and modify your strategies accordingly.

Online stores supported by AI

If you want to make more money with your business, you can also use Playground AI's AI-backed e-commerce feature to create an online store. With AI-based shopping recommendations, personalized product suggestions and smart pricing, you can easily increase sales and revenue for your business. In addition, Playground AI's intelligent machine learning algorithms can help you optimize your store and maximize your profits through automated pricing and marketing strategies.

Technical data services

By harnessing the power of AI, you can also generate additional revenue through data technical services. If you offer services such as AI-based insights, data analytics and machine learning algorithms, you can position yourself as a valuable asset to companies in need of these skills. You can easily find AI-related freelance services on the Internet and offer your services to clients who need them.

Consulting and freelance services

Using Playground AI's network of professionals, you can also offer consulting and freelance services to clients looking for help in properly utilizing the power of AI. Freelance work can range from AI product design to AI-based web development, software programming and more. With Playground AI's worldwide network of professionals, you can easily market yourself and your services, and find clients willing to pay for your expertise.

Using AI-based applications

Finally, you can also make money using AI-driven applications. AI-powered apps can range from automated personal assistant apps to chatbot apps to AI-powered investment apps. By harnessing the power of AI, you can create an app that makes you money with every user. This can be achieved through in-app purchases, ads or a subscription-based model.

Final thoughts

Making money with Playground AI is easy with the right resources and strategies. If you know the different ways to monetize your Playground AI account, you can start earning a steady stream of additional income right out of the box. Whether you want to supplement your income or create a full-time career with Playground AI, this platform offers you the perfect opportunity to make your ideas a reality.

It is a marketable article and it can surely be positioned in Google. It has correct grammar and the keywords are present in a fairly acceptable quantity (without overdoing it or falling short).

Let's see now the step-by-step for you to make money with Playground AI. The URL is https://playgroundai.com/. This is the interface you will find if you are not already registered:

At the top right you can register and then, in the same space, you will find the option to create:

You can create up to 1000 images per day for free and with a commercial license. If you want more, or any of the other advantages, you can use a paid version. Here are the features:

How do you create the images? I love Playground to make or illustrate books, so to decide what images I want I design a book depending on how the publishing market is.

There are large niches that do not disappoint and with which the AI is a marvel: children's, science fiction, fantasy...

The possibilities offered by Playground are many. Let's see some of them, first of all, after clicking on Generate, choose what kind of style you want in the menu at the top left, where it says Filter:

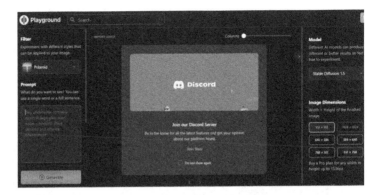

You will find many options, you can use the search engine or try it out. A thousand images a day is enough.

Below, also on the left, you have the *prompt* space. As always, try to be concise and explain what you want, although you can also explore putting just one word or whatever you consider.

I'll show you an example, in Filer I chose Royalistic and my *prompt* was: "I want a scene from a romance novel set in the Victorian era". This is the result:

A bit scary... But it's because of the style chosen and the prompt given. You can get very diverse images.

When writing, keep in mind that, as with all AIs originally created in English (in this book, all except Escríbelo), they understand English better than Spanish. If you don't get the result you would like, you can try using an English *prompt.*

Although the results are getting better and better, there are still some mistakes such as when making people's hands, which do not always have five fingers. And in other "details".

1000 free designs per day with a commercial use license is too powerful not to take advantage of it. Maybe at some point they will turn off the tap, if when you read this you still have this opportunity: take advantage of it to earn money before it's too late.

Give originality to your creations. Find a demand that is not satisfied as well as you could satisfy it and take over the market.

You.com

The last AI specialized in text creation that we will see is You.com:

Its interface is quite simple, you only have to choose above which service you want to use.

Let's start with YouWrite:

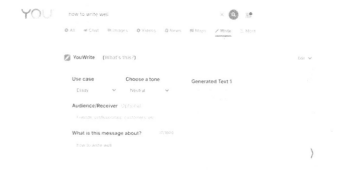

To order the content you have free space for indications, you can choose between five types of tones and six types of texts (titles, essays, articles, publication in social networks...).

In addition to texts, you can also get images (YouImagine), codes (Youcode) and chatbots (Youchat).

I asked him for a cover for this book on YouImagine and this is what he gave me:

The information I gave him was the title and the author's name. The result is a bit weird...

I'm going to ask ChatGPT what this can tell me about You.com to earn money step by step (I didn't ask him about strengths, weaknesses...). The result is this:

You.com is definitely a platform that offers many opportunities to make money online. You.com is an e-commerce platform that allows users to sell products and services online through its online store. Here are the basic steps to make money with You.com:

Create an account on You.com and start exploring its platform and features.
Identify the products or services you wish to sell through You.com. This can include physical or digital products, professional services or anything else you wish to offer.
Create an online store on You.com and start uploading your products or services. Be sure to include detailed descriptions, images and prices for your products.
Start promoting your online store and your products through social networks, email and other online marketing media.
Monitor your sales and revenue, and adjust your marketing and pricing strategies as needed to maximize your revenue.

In terms of the opportunities offered by You.com, one of the biggest opportunities is its large user base and easy-to-use e-commerce platform, which means that you can reach a large audience and sell your products or services effectively. In addition, You.com also offers a wide range of tools and resources to help you promote and sell your products, which means that you don't need to have previous online marketing experience to be successful on You.com.

In summary, You.com is a platform that offers many opportunities to make money online, and by following these basic steps, you can start selling your products or services and generate income online effectively.

I refer to you.com, an artificial intelligence company, to rewrite the text with this in mind.

Of course, I hope I have cleared up the confusion. You.com is an artificial intelligence company that offers a wide range of solutions for the business and financial world. Here are the basic steps to use You.com to make money online:

Register with You.com and familiarize yourself with its platform and artificial intelligence solutions.
Identify what problems or challenges in the business or financial world you are trying to address.
Use You.com's artificial intelligence solutions to help you address these challenges and generate new business opportunities.
Monitor results and adjust your strategies accordingly to maximize your revenue.

As for the advantages of You.com compared to ChatGPT, Escribelo.ia and other similar solutions, one of the biggest advantages is that You.com offers artificial intelligence solutions specific to the world of business and finance. This means that you can get more accurate and relevant results for your business or financial challenges.

In addition, You.com also offers a wide range of tools and resources to help you make the most of its artificial intelligence, which means you don't need to have prior experience in artificial intelligence to be successful with You.com.

In summary, You.com is an artificial intelligence company that offers a wide range of solutions for the world of business and finance, and by following these basic steps, you can start using their artificial intelligence to generate new business opportunities and increase your online revenue.

I would check the result very well. Don't rely too much on AI. Although it ended up being very generic so as not to "get your fingers caught". I'm going to try it with Write it to compare, I have chosen a medium one:

How to Make Money with You.com? Step by Step to Master Artificial Intelligence.
Do you want to maximize your earnings and learn how to make money with You.com? Then you need to learn how to master artificial intelligence. In this article, we present you a step-by-step to learn how to make money with You.com. We will tell you how to get started, how to earn passive income and how to make the most of all the artificial intelligence tools available on You.com.
How to Get Started on You.com: 11 Ways to Make Extra Money.
It doesn't matter how skilled or inexperienced you are in artificial intelligence. There are always ways to start making money with You.com. Here are 11 ways to make extra money working from home:

1. Create your own online store. Retailers can leverage AI-optimized information with targeted offers and personalized products to attract shoppers.

2. Remote consulting. Artificial intelligence experts can offer advice on the best uses of You.com for those who are learning.

3. Sell courses. If you are excellent at artificial intelligence, consider creating a course to help others learn how to make money with You.com.

4. Trading. Are you an expert in the financial market? Then you can use artificial intelligence for trading.

5. Selling photos on the Internet. If you are a professional photographer, you can use You.com to automate and optimize the marketing of your photo sales.

6. Freelance copywriter or digital writer. Use artificial intelligence to make your work more efficient and drive more traffic to your articles.

7. Playing games and earning money on apps. Many gaming apps like Big Time now use artificial intelligence to make games even more exciting.

Domain trading. You can make money buying and selling domains on sites like Namecheap, GoDaddy, Flippa and Dan.com.

9. Affiliate marketing. Affiliate marketing is a great

way to make money online. Use artificial intelligence to optimize your affiliate links and get the best possible results.

10. Microwork online. Finding micro jobs is an excellent way to start making money online. Use artificial intelligence to optimize these jobs to get the best results.

11. Make money with Instagram. Use artificial intelligence to discover affiliate links and mask them so you can trade them safely on Instagram.
Useful Tips to Earn Money with You.com.
Once you have learned the 11 ways to start making money with You.com, it is important to supplement your knowledge with these tips to get the best results:

1. Describe your ideal customer. Artificial intelligence can help you isolate your target market. Learn about your audience's tastes, interests and characteristics to improve your marketing efforts.

Use artificial intelligence to optimize your efforts. Artificial intelligence can help you optimize your marketing efforts by delivering personalized messages, targeted ads and individualized content.

Explore new markets. Use artificial intelligence to search for new markets that you can exploit to increase your profits.

4. Use You.com tools. Use You.com tools to optimize your marketing, reduce costs and increase your online visibility.

5. Invest in intelligent advertising. Use artificial intelligence to help you invest your advertising funds in the best possible way.

6. Market your brand. Use artificial intelligence to help senior managers market their brand to the right customers.

How to Make Money with You.com? The Verdict.

As you can see, there are many ways to start your career with You.com and make money with artificial intelligence. Use these 11 ways and 6 tips to start making money with You.com right now. Maximize your earnings and exploit all the AI tools and resources to the fullest - have incredible success with You.com!

The text is not perfect, for example point 8 is questionable. But it is a basis to have an article ready in a few minutes that can bring value to the reader.

You.com, like Microsoft's new Bing, is one of these next-generation search engines that incorporates AI to not only send you to external content, but also create content based on existing content.

To be able to create texts you need the paid version. The cost is almost ridiculous, they offer you two options, the first for 1 dollar a week (paying 3.99 dollars a month) and the second for 2 (paying 7.99 dollars a month). They have no commitment of permanence, you can pay only one month and if you do not want more you leave it.

The most economical option is 250 submissions with about 25,000 words, the other: 1,000 submissions and about 100,000 words.

Here you have all the information:

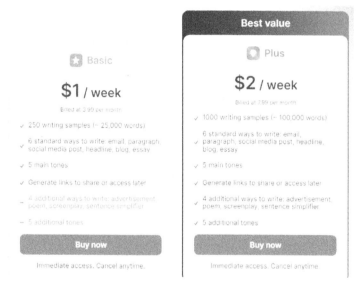

Keep in mind that it is created for texts of a maximum of one thousand words and in English. If your objective is different, such as creating fiction books in Spanish, it may not be the best option.

I think it is an excellent tool for blogs in English or non-fiction books in the same language.

Let's see a little more about images, videos and audios (music) that you can create with AI and sell to make money.

First I want to show you something that might surprise you....

Canva

A program that many people use but few know that it has an integrated AI application. It is very easy to use and works from texts, with the limitation of erotic content (ChatGPT also records erotic, hateful or violent content).

You just have to, as always, click on create a design at the top right and choose what you want:

When you are on the design page, click on Apps at the bottom left:

You just have to describe the design you want it to generate. For example, "a woman and her partner, a robot with artificial intelligence, happy and eating partridge":

This option of offering four versions will also be seen in other AIs such as the following one, this is

Midjourney

An image creator based on Stable Diffusion and offering a beta version to the public from July 2022.

Click or tap on Join the Beta. It sends you to a Discord server, you must make an account to use it. You will be asked for your date of birth to make sure you are over 18. If you are on your phone you may have to download the app. When you log in you will see something like this:

On the left, where it says "newbies", are the free servers (this version offers you limited designs, if you want more you must pay a subscription and you will have access to infinite creations and other advantages such as servers with private chats in which to make and keep your designs; in what you see on the screen you will share space with other users and your publications will be left behind). Click on one of them to start with the designs. You can upload both text and images from which you want your new creations. Below you will see a chat where you can write, put: "/imagine" (without quotes), you will see this:

Click there where it says prompt and then enter what you want.

Is it possible to use Midjourney creations for commercial purposes (i.e.: to make money)?

The answer is only if you are using the paid version.

The designs you generate for free are under a Commons Attribution 4.0 International Non-Commercial Attribution License (https://creativecommons.org/licenses/by-nc/4.0/deed.es) which does not allow the purposes we like.

If you are interested in creating a lot of designs and being able to make a lot of money (as they say in Colombia), consider Midjourney's subscription plans. You can find all the information here:

https://docs.midjourney.com/docs/plans. They are very affordable.

Before creating the first design you will be prompted to accept the terms and conditions, you should know that you give them rights to any file you upload. You will also be able to see some tips and indications to use the platform correctly.

Underneath the four designs that you will get as an answer to your *prompt you* will find something like this:

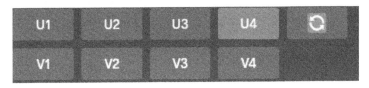

If you want any image just click on V (Variations) and the number of the design, these are counted from top to bottom and from left to right: one is top left, two is top right, three is bottom left and four is bottom right.

To generate the same design in more detail, click on the U (Upscaled) and the design number.

The results it can give you if you put in your own photo are part of Midjourney's success: they have gone viral on social networks.

Uploading a file is very easy, just click on the plus button on the left side of the chat bar.

The menu that you can see on the left is displayed and in which you find the option.

As you can see, it is quite easy to use and interesting.

But this is not the only option. We also have...

Dall-E 2

From the same creators of ChatGPT, Open IA:

To log in you click on Sign Up, you can then click on Login and use the same login as for ChatGPT:

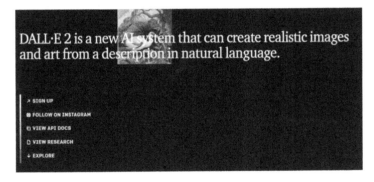

They tell you that you have 50 free credits when you start and then every month you will have 15 more free credits. Each request is one credit. If you want to make more designs you will have to buy credits:

Once inside it is very easy to use, it creates an image from the text you put, it asks for a description. It also allows you to upload an image for editing:

To show you an example I typed "Give me a cover for a book called How to Make Money Online with Artificial Intelligence" and hit the Generate button. This is the result:

Clicking on each design allows you to edit it and get alternative versions. In this case:

Dall-E-2 is especially good at such editing possibilities, you can change only a part of the image, automatically creating a design around it.

When giving the prompts you can get better results if you use English. I am going to show you the result by translating the prompt, "Give me a cover for a book called How to Make Money Online with Artificial Intelligence".

After doing this I have 47 credits, out of the original 50. If I wanted to buy more I would have to pay $15 per 115 credits.

A tip to get the best designs is to tell him to make them in the particular style you are looking for, like a famous painter, for example.

You can ask them to be high quality photos and they will look like that.

Everything you do is saved, you don't lose it when you do more.

And would it be possible to use these creations to make money?

Yes.

Even with the free version?

Yes.

Great point for Dall-E 2.

Other AI

Want more? If you're interested in digging deeper into AI, look for Kaggle and/or Google Colab. I also recommend learning more: edX, GitHub, TutorAI, Stack Overflow, Reddit and the Association for the Advancement of Artificial Intelligence (AAAI). You will be able to find someone to answer any related questions you may have.

There are also more options than those seen in this book which, like everything else, has its limits. If you want to continue exploring options here are some of them; to create or paraphrase texts: Writesonic. To chat: Andi. To create videos from texts: Fliki. To create new images from existing ones, changing the colors, without registration and for free: Palette.fm. If you want to create a professional logo: Looka Logo Maker. To decide the name of your brand or your web domain (you can also use this service to win money, there are websites where you will find contests for names in which you can participate): Namelix. For music: Boomy. One last one for writing: Rytr, it gives you 10 thousand words a month for free.

- Create **music** and monetize it on Spotify and YouTube. You can use Aiva.ai to create the music files. On YouTube you won't have to do anything more than reach the minimum number of users and views to monetize, you can achieve this by using search engine optimization (SEO) techniques and bringing traffic from social networks and/or from a blog positioned in Google. To sell on Spotify you will have to do it with a distributor, you can get a deal that allows you to upload unlimited content for only 12 dollars a year.

- AI **Expert**. Fiverr has already created an option for this new type of professionals. The implementation of AI is generating a lot of work, becoming an expert and helping beginners is a good way to earn money.

- With **data** analytics. You can use Google Cloud AI Platform and/or the service offered by Jeff Bezos' company.

- By converting **speech to text**, you can create subtitles or transform videos into books or articles. One option is Whisper, owned (like ChatGPT and Dall-E) by Open IA.

- **Transcription**. You can narrate your book, speak it and have the AI automatically transform it into text. One of the most popular options for doing this is Apple's Siri. For example, Cipri Quintas, author of *El libro del networking Las 15 claves para relacionarte socialmente con éxito*, acknowledged having created his work in this way.

- You indirectly make money from AI if you sell **through companies that use it**, such as Jeff Bezos' company. Or if you buy **shares of** companies in the sector or related in some way.

- There is a great opportunity in the development of autonomous **drones.**

- Learning an AI **programming** language, such as Python or R. The demand for these professionals is trending.

- Sell your designs on an **image bank** like Adobe Stock or Creative Fabrica, you only have to upload them to the platform once and you can be earning passive income for life.

- **Selling AI-related services** can be done in several ways, we have talked about advertising on *freelance* platforms. The other obvious option is social media (*online* and *offline*), but they are not the only ones. The old method of going door-to-door works. If you want to go digital, try LinkedIn or Instagram. On YouTube you might also find many channels with a contact email. Write them a short, direct message offering a service, including the benefits and price. If you are starting out, consider doing it for free to get experience and testimonials. You could offer them, for example, to create subtitles in English (and other languages). In most cases even the big channels only have the subtitles automatically generated by YouTube in the same language. Contact powerful channels. You could even offer to translate all the content, not just the subtitles: video, audio, descriptions... Look for your customers. It's good to attract them, but don't forget that you can always build a new offer. You must do better than the competition or, the other option: don't have competition. Do something new. The ways to make money with AI are not only the ones in this book, they are endless.

Let's start directly with the step by step:

1 Decide which book to create

The first thing to do is to decide which book to create. To do this you must do market research that includes as a pillar the research of keywords or search terms (*keywords research*).

First, look at the bestseller lists and trends on Google Trends. You must study the demand. Once you have identified an interesting niche because of its high demand, look at the quality of the competition.

Could you make better books than those that are selling well?

Perhaps a more updated manual. A longer and more original novel. A similar content but with a nicer cover...

Look for opportunities.

You can choose a personal branding strategy and focus on creating a business beyond books, with service sales. In that case you will earn more money from the contacts and authority the books give you than from royalties.

You can also choose to use heteronyms or pseudonyms, brands, depending on what you want to publish. No need to show your face or your identity.

Look for what your audience is asking for, check reviews of books that your audience reads, also social networks of content creators that may be similar, what is their audience commenting on?

If they are criticizing something, use it to sell your book.

For example, if they say they liked it, but it was too short, make it clear in the description of your book that it is a full version and have more content than your competition.

Another example: you want to make a book on nutrition. Examine the feedback your buyers have given and it is available online. Maybe for example someone will say something like: I would have liked it if you had some recipes so I could apply the knowledge. And adding some recipes to your book is what will make you a lot of money.

The first step is always market research. It will give you the information you need to create your product.

You can save a lot of time if you use some paid *software*, I recommend Publisher Rocket:

It is a one-time investment for life and in the first book you will most likely get it back. The only limitation is that for now it is only available for three markets: UK, USA and Germany.

According to the creators in the future there will be more stores. It will also stop being a one-time payment, at least for new users, if you buy it when it is still a one-time payment and you will have all the updates for free.

So if you plan to make money with AI by self-publishing books, check if it's still a fee or how much it costs; it's a very easy to use and very powerful tool.

There are different types of books, one of the most common divisions being low *content* books and *high content books*.

In addition, there are books with zero content: notebooks, diaries and other blank or colored books. Without an interior differentiated only by their format.

Low-content books are coloring books, mazes, crossword puzzles... They are made by designers rather than writers. They are the cheapest to produce and, therefore, among which there is more competition and, due to the ease of making them, little room for differentiation.

It is very difficult not to be, for example, a crossword book just like all other crossword books.

It is possible, of course. Humor works very well to achieve it. Originality is key in any business.

High content books are those that require more investment. They are longer.

This typology is not exact. Over time, non-fiction type books are getting shorter and shorter and with that you have less content.

I like high content. To make books of extreme value. Where, like this one, I pour my life to give a piece of truth.

Understand that AI is a writing assistant. Don't just copy and paste without providing any value.

To make money you must positively impact the lives of others. The more you do this, the more money you will make.

High content or low content books?

The answer depends on your profile - are you more comfortable in Word or in Canva and Playground AI?

You know, if you like writing and proofreading, do high-content books. If graphic design is your thing, do everything low content.

In my case, as you can see, I like the high content and I will explain my method for this type of book in its two main versions: fiction and non-fiction.

2. Create your book with AI

For non-fiction consider using Write It and split the book with articles, adding narration done with ChatGPT and/or by hand.

If your thing is fiction and you want a novel you can use the famous step by step hero's journey or even follow scene by scene what screenwriters do according to William Blake's manual: *Save the cat*.

For books with low content and illustrations you can use Playground AI.

There are many formulas. This is like cooking. Make sure it has the ingredients you decide on and that it makes sense, take care of the thread, and make sure you deliver on what matters most to your readers.

If they are romance books perhaps the love story is what you should take care of the most. If it's a manual, get them to solve their problem. If it's erotica, titillate. If it is a joke book, make them laugh.

Give the AI all the information so they know what you want and how they can do it, tell them what they have access to, such as public domain books.

Here is a small example, at the end it collapsed, but it could be a base to edit and with a *prompt* that includes the information about the past history and the objectives, it could be expanded as you wish.

act as if you were the best thriller writer in history, give me a text with a good cliffhanger, a good story that a young female audience can empathize with.

"Emma's life seemed perfect: a successful job as a lawyer, a loving boyfriend and a group of loyal friends. But everything changed when she received a strange phone call in the middle of the night. The voice on the other end of the phone was accusing her of something she hadn't done.

Desperate to discover the truth, Emma began to investigate on her own and quickly realized that nothing was what it seemed. Every answer raised more questions and every person she met seemed to have something to hide.

Emma found herself caught in a web of lies and dark secrets that were dragging her into a dangerous game of cat and mouse. But when she started receiving threats in her own home, she knew she had to uncover the truth before it was too late.

However, when Emma finally found out who was behind it all, she realized that the person she trusted the most might be her worst enemy. Who can you trust when everything you know is at stake?

The room fell silent as Emma hung up the phone. Heart pounding, she realized that the only person she could trust was herself. But would she be up to what lay ahead? She would have the answer to that question in a single sentence: Emma was alone and in danger, not knowing who to trust on a dark night..."

give me a cliffhanger

"Emma stopped dead in her tracks when she heard a noise behind her. Without moving, she held her breath and listened carefully. Was it just her imagination or was someone there? Then, a figure emerged from the darkness and Emma knew she was not alone. In a barely audible whisper, a voice said, "I'm sorry, Emma. There's nowhere to go." Emma gasped, knowing that her life would never be the same after what happened next..."

the story continues

Emma tried to run, but her legs felt like lead. The figure was getting closer and closer, its intentions unknown. Emma desperately searched for a weapon or something to defend herself with, but there was nothing within reach.

Just as the figure was about to reach her, Emma closed her eyes and prepared for the worst. But instead of feeling the impact of an attack, she felt a gentle hand on her shoulder. She opened her eyes to find herself facing a man with a mask on his face.

"Don't be afraid," said the unfamiliar voice behind the mask. "It is I, your friend. I have come to help you."

Emma was stunned - who could her friend be dressed like that and why was he there? The figure handed her a note and disappeared into the darkness before Emma could say a single word. With trembling hands, she opened the note and read:

"I know what you're researching. I know what you have discovered. But you must be careful. Not everything is what it seems. Trust no one, even those you trust the most. Your life depends on it."

Emma was terrified - what had she discovered that would put her in danger? Who could be behind it all? With more questions than answers, Emma knew her adventure of discovering the truth had only just begun.

go on, add a policeman (as if it were a crime and police novel), make it take place in Madrid and show some known scenery.

Emma felt overwhelmed by everything that was happening, but she knew she had to stay calm and find some way to protect herself. With a little research, she discovered that there was a policeman in Madrid who specialized in cases like hers. His name was Alvaro Garcia, and he was known to be cunning and relentless in solving crimes.

Emma decided to contact Inspector Garcia and explained everything that had happened. Although he was initially reluctant to help her, Garcia agreed to listen to her story and promised to investigate the case.

Together, Emma and Garcia began to investigate and uncovered a web of corruption and crime that stretched further than they could have ever imagined. They followed leads throughout Madrid, including the neighborhoods of Chamberí and La Latina, and visited well-known places such as Retiro Park and Plaza Mayor.

As they got deeper and deeper into the investigation, Emma and Garcia realized that they were being watched and that their lives were in danger. However, they were determined to uncover the truth and bring justice, despite the dangers they faced.

On a dark and stormy night, Emma and Garcia arrived at an abandoned building on the outskirts of Madrid. There, they confronted those responsible for all the evil they had investigated. It was an epic battle, and when all seemed lost, an unexpected turn of events changed everything.

Who triumphed in the struggle between good and evil? Did Emma and Garcia succeed in uncovering the truth and bringing justice? The answers to these questions and many more await you in the next installment of this thrilling suspense story.

It continues with a Colombian girl and a trip to Medellin. I want a scene with the Medellin Cartel partying in lleras park, in Poblado, the policeman falls in love with the Colombian girl, suspense with romance.

After the intense investigations in Madrid, Emma and Garcia decide to travel to Medellin, Colombia, in search of more clues about the case. There, they meet a young Colombian woman named Maria, who turns out to be key in uncovering the truth.

Maria takes them to a luxurious neighborhood in Poblado, where the famous Lleras Park, the heart of Medellin's nightlife, is located. There, the three attend a party given by the feared Medellin Cartel, and find themselves in the middle of a dangerous and exciting environment at the same time.

Garcia, who had been focused on his work and had kept his heart closed, begins to feel an irresistible attraction to Maria. As they investigate and follow leads, Garcia and Maria get to know each other better and begin to fall in love.

But, at the same time, the tension continues to grow as they get closer and closer to the truth about the case. Emma, Garcia and Maria discover that they are in the eye of the hurricane, and that the truth could put their lives in danger.

The plot becomes increasingly tense, and the three find themselves in a race against time to uncover the truth before it's too late. Will Garcia and Maria manage to survive and escape together with their love intact, or will they fall victim to the clutches of the cartel and the hidden truth? Will Emma, Garcia and Maria manage to unravel the mysteries and bring justice, or will they be defeated by the darkness that surrounds them? The answer to these questions and many more in the next installment of this thrilling suspense story with touches of romance.

I want an action scene with mobsters and cops in Poblado where the theme of state corruption and the love between García, a Spaniard, and María, a Colombian, paisa (from Medellín), cultural differences and a funny dialogue or joke, appear

The scene begins with Garcia, Maria and Emma chasing a suspect in the streets of Poblado, Medellin. The mobsters are following them closely, and the tension is at its peak.

Suddenly, Garcia and Maria break away from Emma to follow their suspect, and find themselves face to face with a group of armed mobsters. The tension is palpable as Garcia and Maria prepare for a fight.

Garcia: "Hands up!" exclaims Garcia, pointing his gun at the mobsters.

Maria: "You say that as if you know how to speak Spanish," Maria replies with a wry smile.

Garcia: "Well, I hope they at least understand the language of guns," Garcia replies with a nervous smile.

The scene becomes action-packed when the cops arrive to the rescue and engage the gangsters in an intense battle. During the fight, Garcia and Maria demonstrate their bravery and combat skills, and manage to escape from the gangsters.

But the tension continues to grow when they discover that state corruption is behind it all, and that some police officers are working with the gangsters. Garcia and Maria must work together to uncover the truth and bring justice.

As the scene progresses, the chemistry between Garcia and Maria becomes more and more evident, and they see themselves reflected in the cultural differences that separate them. But through it all, their love and determination to do justice prevails.

Garcia: "You know, being a Spanish policeman in Colombia is like being a vegan in a slaughterhouse".

Maria: "And being a paisa in Spain?"

Garcia: "It's like being a bullfighter at an animal rights demonstration".

Maria laughs, and the two look into each other's eyes, knowing that together they can overcome any obstacle. The scene ends with a passionate kiss and a mysterious cliffhanger that leaves the viewer waiting for the next installment.

What's that cliffhanger, give it to me in the style of Stephen King.

The cliffhanger ends with Garcia and Maria running to Lleras Park, in Poblado, to confront the leaders of the Medellin cartel. Tension mounts as they approach the mafia leader's mansion, and uncertainty hangs in the air.

Suddenly, a door opens and a dark figure appears in the doorway. Garcia and Maria point their guns, ready for action.

"Who are you?" asks Garcia in a firm voice.

The figure does not respond, and an eerie silence envelops the scene. Garcia and Maria stare at the figure, waiting for its next move.

And then, suddenly, the figure lunges toward them, and the screen goes black.

"The battle for justice and love has never been so intense," says a voiceover. "Who will survive the confrontation with the Medellín cartel? Will Garcia and

Maria be able to take on the corruption and emerge victorious? Find out the answer in the next installment of this thrilling tale of love and suspense."

I want a party between the Colombian mafia and the Russian mafia, show me how the characters go from Medellín to Guatapé and enjoy life, make jokes and there is a lot of romance between the couple that lives a kind of honeymoon, explain what happens with all the characters and close possible plots and questions that we have opened before.

The party between the Colombian mafia and the Russian mafia is an event full of luxury and excess. Garcia and Maria, hand in hand, find themselves surrounded by important and dangerous people, but they are too busy enjoying each other to worry about the dangers around them.

The night passes without incident, and García and María decide to escape from the party to enjoy a few days of peace and quiet. They travel to Guatapé, a beautiful and joyful place, and begin to enjoy their time together.

During their days in Guatapé, García and María visit El Peñol Park, one of the region's most popular tourist attractions, and encounter a group of foreign tourists. Something about one of them catches Garcia's attention, but he cannot identify what exactly it is.

However, Garcia and Maria are not sidetracked by their suspicions and decide to enjoy their time together. They stroll around town, sampling the delicious local food and cracking jokes and banter. Night falls and Garcia and Maria find themselves sitting on the shore of the lake, enjoying the scenery and their newfound love.

Suddenly, the tranquility of the night is interrupted by a scream. Garcia and Maria rush to investigate, and discover that the group of tourists they had seen earlier is being robbed by thieves. Garcia acts quickly, using his skills as a policeman to stop the thieves and protect the tourists.

In the end, Garcia and Maria discover that the tourist who had caught their attention was actually a federal agent in disguise, and that the night had been a trap to catch the thieves. Garcia and Maria are recognized

You will have to edit the result, but it should not take as much time as writing it from scratch.

Once you have it you can publish it, you will only need a cover that you can make very quickly and easily with Canva.

3 Publish your book

Where to publish? In D2D. It is an aggregator that distributes your book in the world's largest ecommerce and other electronic bookstores, both the electronic version (*ebook*) and the paper version (paperback).

The process is simple, but do it carefully. You will need to include as many search terms as you can and provide a description. Of course, you already know which AI to use to write it.

4 Promotion

Sell it cheaper for a limited time to make a launch strategy. If you have an email list, social networks, a channel or group on Telegram, use it. If you don't have one yet, create one and include a free gift in your book in exchange for entering. This way you will be creating an audience to send your next books to and each one will have more impact than the previous one.

Other books that may interest you

Passive Income and Investing for Beginners: How to Really Make Money Online from Home While you Sleep, Personal Finance and Business Strategy

Investing in the Stock Market for Smart Beginners: Easy Guide to Make Money Online From Home With Passive Income and Enjoy Financial Freedom With Dividends (Stocks for the Long run)

The Secret Method of Digital Marketing and Sales for Entrepreneurs: The Business Strategy Handbook for Successful Entrepreneurship Today Without a big Budget

The Black Book of Seduction : 17 Psychological Tricks To Talk, Conquer, Fall in Love, Manipulate and Dominate Men and Women + Flirting Phrases

Thank you very much for making it to the end.

We hope you had a good time.

We would be very grateful for a review and for you to recommend this reading to anyone you think might find it helpful.

Made in the USA
Las Vegas, NV
18 June 2025